Explore

Fascinating Facts for Young Learners.

By Author Jamie Pedrazzoli

All rights reserved, Copyright 2023© by Jamie Pedrazzoli AKA Author Jamie Bach

Copyright fuels creativity. Thank you for buying an authorized edition of this book and complying with the copyright laws by not reproducing, scanning, or distributing any part of this book in any form without permission. To contact the author for permissions email pedrazzolij@yahoo.com.

ISBN: 9798389184480

This book is dedicated to my beautiful daughters.

The names in this book are used fictitiously and any resemblance of persons is coincidental. The facts in this book are based on information provided to the author.

I attempted to put the sound of foreign words in parenthesis to help you pronounce them easier.

Please remember that I speak English so I am attempting to help others pronounce the words by the way I hear them.

"Hola. Me llamo Pablo. (Oh-la Me-Yah-moe Pah-blow) or "Hello, my name is Pablo."

I live in the Chiapas Highlands where there is a lot of farming.

I live in an Ejido (ee-hee-doe) which is a piece of farmland used for agriculture owned by a group of citizens. We each own a section of this farm which makes it more affordable.

I have dos hermanos (dos- err-mah-noes) or two siblings. Do you have any brothers or sisters?

I have a burro (boo-roe) or donkey which helps me do some of my chores.

Se llama es marrón (say-yah-mah-ess-grees) or he is called Brown.

What is there to do near me?

We have wine-tasting tours, ATV adventures, shopping, and restaurants.

The town of Mexicali is near me as well. There are zoos, museums, casinos, shopping malls, and hot springs there.

I want to tell you about some Mexican history.

In 1500 B.C. the Olmec people lived in the area that is now Tabasco and Veracruz. They cultivated crops and built large monuments that can still be seen today.

Next, the Mayan Indians thrived in Mexico around 250 A.D.

The Mayans had *hieroglyphic writing, studied mathematics, and made pottery. They were a very advanced society.

*A hieroglyph is a picture or symbol that represents a word.

Next came the Toltecs. They lived in central Mexico between 600-900 A.D. They were known to have powerful armies. Their capital city was called Tula or Tollan.

In 1325 A.D. the Aztec Indians arrived in the Valley of Anahuac and settled near lake Texcoco. Their first emperor was named Itzcoatl.

The Aztec city of Tenochtitlan (tay-nok-tah-lahn) was built in the middle of a lake. It was estimated that over 200,000 people lived there. Today, unfortunately, most of present-day Mexico City was built overtop their ancient ruins.

In 1519 Hernán Cortés arrived in Mexico to claim the land for the country of Spain.

The Aztec leader Montezuma II thought that Cortés was one of their gods because of his pale skin. He opened his kingdom to all the new white strangers.

The Spanish took him hostage and destroyed much of the city of Tenochtitlan.

In 1810 Father Miguel Hidalgo encouraged Native Mexicans to revolt against the Spanish rulers.

In 1821 Mexico won its freedom from Spain.

In 1829 Spain tried to recapture Mexico.

In 1833 Santa Anna becomes the president after leading a successful resistance against Spain.

On May 12, 1846, the United States and Mexico began to fight over the state of Texas. The United States declared war. A treaty was signed when General Winfield Scott captured Mexico City. This treaty was called the Treaty of Guadalupe Hidalgo and it was signed on February 2, 1848.

Texas, New Mexico, and California were given to the US as part of this treaty.

In 1863 the French invaded Mexico.

In 1877 a revolt took place and Porfirio Díaz took control of Mexico. He ruled as a dictator until 1911.

In 1910 Francisco Madero called a revolution against Díaz.

In 1913 Madero is overthrown and there are many riots.

In 1920 Alvero Obregón becomes President and the revolution ended.

Now I want to tell you about some Mexican food.

We have a custard dish with caramel sauce on it called flan. I like to enjoy this dish on special occasions.

I'm sure you have probably heard of tacos. Am I right? Those are meat-filled shells.

What about guacamole (gwah-kah-moe-lay)? Have you heard of that? It is an avocado dip.

We use bread called tortillas (tor-tee-yahs) for many of our dishes. Tortillas are flatbreads made of wheat or corn.

What about nachos? Have you tried those? Nachos are chips made from tortilla bread with cheese drizzled on top.

Hot chocolate was a sacred drink to the Aztec Indians. We still enjoy this drink today.

Another native dish is a corn dough stuffed with meats, cheeses, or fruits and veggies called a tamale (tah-mah-lay).

Mole (moh-lay) is a sauce that has over 20 ingredients in it. Sometimes it is made with sweet fruits and chocolate.

Elote(ee-low-tay) is probably known as corn on the cob to you and it is one of my favorite snacks.

For breakfast, we usually have chilaquiles (chee-lah-key-lays) which are corn tortillas with scrambled eggs, salsa, sour cream, cheese, and sometimes pulled chicken on top.

It is served with frijoles (free-hole-ays) or refried beans.

Next, I will tell you about some Mexican culture.

Have you heard of a Piñata (pin-yah-tah)? That is a decorated figure or animal that is filled with candy or toys.

We often have these at parties and children take turns hitting them with a bat.

In Mexico, we like to do the Jarabe Tapatia (har-ah-bee-tah-pah-tee-uh) or the 'Hat Dance.' This dance is complicated and illustrates the courtship between men and women.

We often wear traditional outfits for celebrations.

The Sombrero (som-bray-roh) is a wide-brimmed hat.

Serapes (sah-rah-pays) are shawls or blankets that many people like to wear.

The China Poblana (chee-nah-poh-blah-no) is a beautifully decorated skirt with a white blouse worn during festivals.

The Charro (chah-row) is a cowboy-like outfit that men wear.

Mariachi (mah-ree-ah-chee) is a style of Mexican music that dates to the 18th century.

They play musical instruments and sing many songs, usually about love.

We celebrate the Three Kings Day or Dia de los Santos Reyes (celebrates baby Jesus), Carnival, Cinco de Mayo, Mexican Independent Day, Christopher Columbus Day, Día de Muertos (similar to Halloween), and Christmas.

What is the school like in Mexico?

The Primaria School (primary) is for grades 1 through 6. We are taught to learn English or French as a second language.

The Secundaria School (Secondary) is a Middle school that consists of grades 7 through 9. We learn world history, physics, chemistry, art, and literature.

The Preparatoria Escuela (High School) consists of grades 10 through 12.

There are many colleges in Mexico, especially in the cities.

Public school is free, however, the average number of children who complete school in Preparatoria is rare. Many children quit school to work on their parents' farms.

Well, I must get back to work on our farm. Adiós (ah-dee-ohs) or Goodbye.

Hola. Me llamo Dulce. (Oh-la Me- Yah-moe Dull-say) or "Hello, my name is Dulce."

I speak Spanish language, which is the official language of Mexico. Do you speak any Spanish?

I live in Acapulco (ah-kah-pull-koe) Mexico. It is a beach town on the Pacific Coast. It is known as the city behind the cliffs.

My Country calls itself the Estados Unidos Mexicanos (Es-tah-does-oo-nee-dos-mey-hee-cah-noes) or the United Mexican States.

Mexico is made up of 31 states.

Where is the country of Mexico located?

It is the Southernmost nation in North America.

Mexico, mi pais (me pah-eez) or my country has many different landscapes.

There are mountains to the North and East, deserts to the West, and rainforests to the South. Most of the big cities are in Southern Mexico.

Our capital city is called Mexico City.

The climate is different depending on where you are in Mexico.

The average temperature in Acapulco where I live is 86 degrees Fahrenheit (30 degrees Celsius).

In the city of Madera in the state of Chihuahua, the temperature is about 67 degrees Fahrenheit (19.4 degrees Celsius).

Speaking of Chihuahuas, do you know what they are?

If you said a small dog, then you are correct!

I have one for a pet. His name is Chaco.

What type of Government do we have here in Mexico?

We have The Presidential Republic with Federal Structure.

The Constitution divides the Government into The Executive, Legislative, and Judicial branches.

The head of the State or the President is elected by voters.

The major religion in Mexico is Christianity.

The Mexican currency is called the Peso.

One Peso is equal to .055 USD.

The Mexican flag is green, white, and red. There is an Eagle on a cactus with a snake in its beak in the center of the flag. That is the Mexican Coat of Arms and it comes from the Ancient Aztec Indians.

The green in our flag stands for hope. The white stands for unity. The red stands for the blood of the heroes.

So, what is there to do in Acapulco where I live?

We have cliff diving, zip lines, beautiful beaches, horseback riding, snorkeling, diving, and many museums.

Do you think you would ever dive off of a cliff?

We also have Mexico's largest port here in my hometown.

I want to tell you about a few more things people come to Mexico to see.

Chichén Itzá (cheet-zen-eat-zah) is a beautiful Ancient pyramid built by the Mayan Indians. This is a huge tourist attraction.

Three rivers meet and create the Agua Azul (ah-gwah-ah-sool) Waterfalls. People like to come here and swim in the gorgeous blue waters.

An island off of the town of Cancún (can-coon) called Isla Mujeres (ees-lah-moo-hair-es) is known for snorkeling.

The city of Cancún is recognized for being a Spring Break retreat full of many hotels.

The underground river of Cenote Angelita (say-no-tay-an-hay-lee-tah) is a famous place for scuba divers to visit.

There is a beautiful hidden beach located in the Marieta Islands that tourists take a boat to reach.

Here is a photo of me at Marieta Island.

I want to talk to you about some of the animals in Mexico.

We have grey whales, manatees, manta rays, and dolphins in the sea.

We have many birds here such as parrots and eagles. The caracara is the National Bird.

We have over 700 different reptile species here some of those include iguanas and lizards.

This is a photo of an iguana. Have you ever seen one of these?

There are about 430 mammals here some of which include the jaguar, puma, and many different monkeys.

I will now leave you with some words in the Spanish language.

Hello – Hola (oh-lah)

Goodbye – Adiós (ah-dee-ohs)

Bird – Pájaro (pah-har-oh)

Jungle – Selva (sel-vah)

House – Casa (cah-sah)

Thank you – Gracias (grah-see -as)

Goodnight – Buenas noches (bway-nos-no-chess)

Friend – Amiga (ah-mee-gah) for a girl

Amigo (ah-mee-goh) for a boy

Thanks for exploring Mexico with us.

Adiós or Goodbye.

THE END.

Here is a bonus photo of traditional Mexican clothing.

Other books in this series include:

Exploring Romania

Exploring Ireland

Exploring Costa Rica

Exploring New Zealand

Exploring Germany

Exploring Zambia

Other books in the Around the World Series include:

Denmark

India

Romania

Costa Rica

Vietnam

Zambia

Germany

Jordan

The Philippines

Ireland

Mexico

Japan

South Africa

Ukraine

New Zealand

Please support me as an author by checking out my other books available under Jamie Bach. My books can be purchased online at most online bookstores.

For kids and young adults

Tongue-twisting alphabet fun with Koby Jack and Bogart

Counting shapes and color fun with Koby Jack and Bogart

My Jungle Adventure in Costa Rica

Jess the Fox (also in Spanish) Jess el Zorro

Florida girls

Florida girls 2

Let's learn sight words Kindergarten

<u>**For Adults or Teens**</u>

Aleida Orphan no more a Cinderella story with a twist

Words of encouragement and how to cope with what life brings you

Untrusting Eyes

School for the Enchanted

About the Author

Jamie Pedrazzoli (Jamie Bach) grew up in Vero Beach Florida where she spent time taking art classes in high school with the Center for the Arts Museum. She always enjoyed reading and writing.

She has three daughters that help inspire her to write.

"I'm so glad I can share my books with the world; I hope everyone enjoys reading them".

Check out her website and other links to social media.

Author site on Facebook

https://www.facebook.com/jamiebachauthorchildrensbooks

Author sites

http://authorjamiebach.weebly.com

http://zolibooks.weebly.com

Twitter

https://twitter.com/jamiebach421

Adventure Blog

http://theadventuresofkobyjackandbogart.weebly.com

Instagram

https://www.instagram.com/jamiepedrazzoliauthor

http://www.instagram.com/jamiebach421author

Remember if you wish to contact this author an email address is provided. Do not call her or her parents' home. This is an invasion of privacy and is not appreciated. If it is of urgent importance EMAIL is the best way.

That email is pedrazzolij@yahoo.com

Have an adult help you cut out the collectible bookmark to use while reading this book.

Made in the USA
Middletown, DE
28 September 2023